Praise for Birdie Jaworski

Her posts draw more than 1,000 hits a day from readers fascinated by the woman who buys antiwrinkle cream for her pet monkey Hubert or by the wife who orders Bust-Sculpt Contouring ointment for her husband, who ingests it as an alternative to Viagra.

- Time Magazine

What Birdie discovered about people – and herself – went more than skin deep.

- Positive Thinking Magazine

Birdie Jaworski, an Avon Products Inc. representative in rural Las Vegas, N.M., has developed one of the most popular blogs hosted at news web site Salon.com ... One reason for Ms. Jaworski's popularity: her unvarnished reviews of Avon products, which she tries before peddling to customers.

- Wall Street Journal

100 Ways to Recruit AVON Representatives

by Birdie Jaworski

Gallinas Girls Publishing
Las Vegas, New Mexico

This book is dedicated to every Avon Lady who still seeks new friends, new money for her pocket, new memories by knocking on strange doors. I still sell Avon, and my heart knows your joys, your struggle.

Much love from Birdie

Also by Birdie Jaworski

Don't Shoot! I'm Just the Avon Lady

100 Ways to Sell AVON

My Tiny Vegas

GALLINAS: Sixteen Months with a Biweekly Magazine Featuring the Arts, Cultures and Communities of Northeastern New Mexico

And look for *How to Keep your Avon Recruits* coming soon!

Table of Contents

Introduction

I wrote a check for ten dollars, made it out to "Avon." My hand jolted a bit, making the "v" look a little like an "n." Anon. My new district manager slipped it into her leather valise and shook my hand. Her Avon faux emerald and sterling silver ring cut into my flesh, leaving a slight dent in my palm.

"You made a great decision, Birdie. Call me if you have questions. And remember the power of three!"

I stared at the pile of ten shiny brochures for a long time. The power of three. I already forgot what it meant, forgot that I should talk to three people a day, offer three lipsticks, three chances for another stay-at-home mom to make some money. The blue binder housing the Avon bible contained this information, but it would be days before I would open it.

Selling Avon was scarier than bungie jumping, more terrifying than arranging a blind date, as deep-mind challenging as any algebra exam. The first few weeks I didn't stand on anyone's front porch with confidence, didn't wait for my potential customer to answer her door. I dropped a stamped Avon brochure and one fragrance sample on each stoop, pressed the button and ran like hell. Sometimes I hid behind bushes to watch what my neighbors would do. They usually looked right, then left, glanced at my name on the back of the book, then tried to figure out how that strange lady with the two little boys and tie-dyed t-shirt could run so fast.

Avon works the way many other stay-at-home businesses do, through a combination of direct sales and recruiting efforts. Some representatives simply sell product to friends and family. Others spend long evenings sitting at the local coffee house, meeting one potential downline after another. Avon stressed that either approach was acceptable, but that the real rewards come through building a solid base of hard-working ambitious representatives beneath you, each of whom filled your pockets whenever they sold a lotion or recruited another lotion-seller.

For most businesses that offer a multi-level approach, recruiting other like-minded folks can offer huge rewards. Avon is no exception. Selling Avon is fun! You not only get Avon's wonderful products at a discount, you get to share them with others and make money doing so! Why not open your business to include other Avon Reps, women and men who will work with you, and work with each other, helping to show anyone that there is an opportunity to share beauty, love, hard work, and a little bit of silliness and fun available to them? I bet you'll be glad that you did!

Enjoy these 100 ways to recruit Avon Representatives, and have fun putting into practice the sample scripts and ideas I've shared with you.

YOU can do it. I believe in you.

Online Videos Are HOT!

1. Videos: Online videos are HOT! Start a You Tube or Vimeo channel and make short films highlighting your successful Avon business. How about a video titled "*Turning Deodorant Into Dollars*" or "*3 Easy Ways To Demonstrate Men's Cologne.*" If you show prospective Avon Reps how easy it is for YOU to share your beauty expertise, they will know that they can do it, too!

"Turn Deodorant into Dollars!"

Befriend Your Realtor!

2. Ask your Realtor to include your business card and information in the Welcome Neighbor packette they give to new homeowners. Buying a home is a big financial commitment - perhaps an Avon business can help lighten the load!

Welcome Home! Let me help you start your home-based business!

Visit the Farmers' Market!

3. Farmers' Markets can be a wonderful place to generate recruiting leads. Bring samples of your Avon products and some brochures. Stop at each booth and speak to every farmer, baker, and crafts-person. Often these entrepreneurs are looking for ways to enhance their income.

"Avon Can Help Your Income GROW!"

It's Always the Season to Share AVON!

4. A great place to advertise that you are building your Avon business is in your church bulletin! Many places of worship have a weekly newsletter that is given to participants during fellowship. Your payment or donation for your listing will go to a good cause.

Let your faith community know you sell AVON!

Every Race Needs a Pretty Face!

5. Sponsor a runner or a cyclist in a big race! They will wear your name and contact info on their singlet. As they cross the finish line, you are a winner, too!

"Be a Winner Too!"

Teach an Online Class!

6. Online classes can be fun and lucrative! Offer to teach a free workshop - perhaps *"How to Earn Money at Home"* or *"Lipstick Success."* Create a few electronic handouts that students can download at the end of the class. You can teach using a chatroom, a forum at your website or blog, or through email.

"How to Earn Money at Home!"

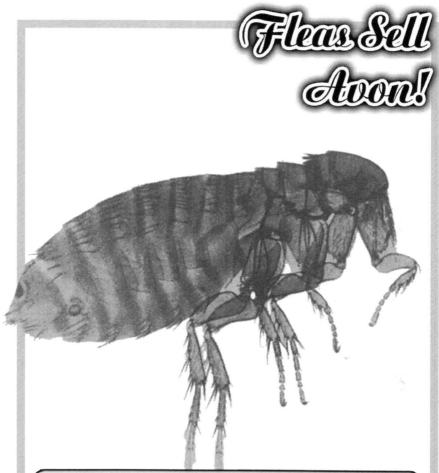

Fleas Sell Avon!

7. Who knows fleas better than an animal vet? Avon's flagship product - Skin So Soft - is renowned as an insect repellent, and works wonderfully on dogs and cats as flea kryptonite. Vets make wonderful Avon Reps - they can recommend Skin So Soft as a safe, non-chemical alternative to poisonous flea treatments. Vets also interact with hundreds of pet owners a week, and can quickly build their own Avon team of Flea Fightin' Superheroes!

Recruit a flea-fighting superhero!

Button Up!

Need Ca$h?

8. Wear buttons with cute phrases: "Looking For Beauty?" or "Need Ca$h?" or "I'm Looking For a Few Good Women!" Make sure you keep a smile on your face while you are out and about!

"I'm Looking For a Few Good Women!"

Network!

9. Network through local business channels: Every town and city has a Better Business Bureau, a Chamber of Commerce, a Kiwanis, or other business fraternal organizations. Get to know your neighborhood business people through the gatherings, coffee hours, and events your local organizations host. Many folks are experiencing tough business times these days and are looking at ways to expand their own business or create a new income stream. You will reap the benefit of finding reps who already have sales and business experience!

Find Reps who Have Experience!

10. Salute Our Military! Military bases are a wonderful source of Avon Reps! Stationed personnel often have spouses who have been relocated and are now looking for work. Visit the places near your local base where partners may shop or frequent - coffee shops, groceries, child care centers - and ask if you can leave a stack of Avon brochures, business cards, and flyers. Give callers a free set of samples or a small gift product, and invite them to hear about the Avon opportunity.

"Thank you for your service to our country. Let me treat you to Avon."

Invest in a Vanity Phone Number!

11. Your information may come across someone's attention, but maybe she doesn't have a pen and paper to write down your contact info! Or maybe she writes it down and loses it, or forgets whose number it is. What a disaster! Not so if you have a vanity number. You can sign up for a free number through Google Voice or a low cost number through Skype if you like. Try to find a combination that will allow you to use words and numbers to get you message across: CALL-AVON or 123-AVON.

"Call Me - 123-AVON!"

Meetup With Folks in Your Area!

®

Meetup

12. Meetup.com offers hundreds of exciting get-togethers in your area. Do you like Sci-Fi movies? Book clubs? Writing? Philosophy? Join a Meetup group and meet people face-to-face in your community who are of like mind. Meetups always have time for folks to exchange personal information. Let your fellow writers or philosophers or singers or dancers know that you sell Avon and are looking for others to sell Avon with you.

Your love of Sci-Fi, or books or cooking is an asset!

Throw a Party!

13. Host an Avon Party at your own home or at a customer's home, or host one for your newest recruit! Spread out samples, demonstration products, and lots of colorful Avon brochures. Make sure to offer makeovers & door prizes. This is a great way to generate customers, but don't forget to send every party goer home with a flyer that explains how Avon is a fantastic company with an incredible earnings opportunity. Collect names & email addresses at the party and follow up w/your newsletter.

Offer Makeovers & Door Prizes!

Tell the Media!

14. Don't dismiss this tried and true technique! Write a short-and-to-the-point press release about your growing Avon business. Mention how many customers you have, how many folks are in your Leadership team, and what customers can expect to see in the upcoming Avon brochures. Send your release to local media and the beauty blogs.

Write a press release!

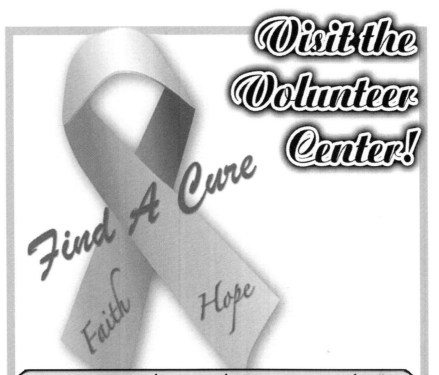

Visit the Volunteer Center!

Find A Cure

Faith

Hope

15. Does your city have a Volunteer Center? These groups collect names of organizations looking for volunteers and those folks in the community who are looking to spend time helping others. Speak with the Center management, and let them know that your Avon Leadership team is involved in charitable work. Give some examples of the ways in which your team has helped others - perhaps by organizing a Breast Cancer Walk for the Cure, or through Fundraising efforts. Ask if they know anyone who may need extra income in addition to a place on a team that is committed to helping the community.

Let your community know you care - AND sell Avon!

Give a Band a Hand!

16. Sponsor a local band - dance, country western, even a Baroque quartet. The band can hoist your banner across the stage. "Give This Band a Hand - we did, we're Avon!" Don't forget to add your contact info!

Music isn't only the food of love - it can help put food on your table too!

Really Clean Up with Avon!

17. Laundromat owners may be looking for some additional income. Bring them onto your team, and show them how they can offer Avon right through their laundromat to their existing customers. They can display Avon jewelry and body care products as well as makeup. A laundromat is a great place to meet folks who could use another income source as well, so your new laundry recruit will have a ready stream of potential downline members.

Avon at the Laundromat!

Avon on the Internet Air!

18. Podcasting: Start your own Avon Biz radio show! Record a regular five-minute podcast where you tell your own downline how to increase their Avon sales. Make sure to add funny sound effects and cool background music. Encourage your sales team to share your podcasts with interested parties. Remember: When your downline recruits, YOU recruit!

When Your Downline Recruits, YOU Recruit!

Have a Magnetic Personality!

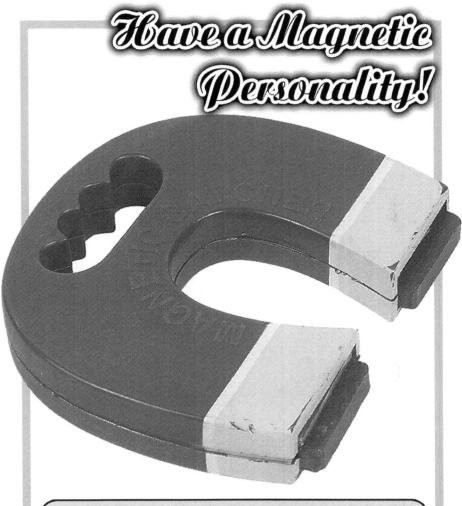

19. Put your car to work! Have magnetic signs made for your car that promote your Avon business and the Avon sales opportunity. *"Buy or Sell Avon - Call Me!"* Make sure your signs are large enough for folks to read from across the street. I've even seen these offered in the Avon sales tool catalogue from time to time!

"Buy or Sell Avon - Call Me!"

Sponsor an Event!

20. Little League, Girl Scouts - find a non-profit organization that resonates with you and sponsor an event!
Helping with a community event fosters goodwill and will
get you noticed by other business people. You will get
your logo or tagline on the event's advertising, so use it
to your advantage - make sure you mention that you not
only sell Avon, but that you help others sell it, too!

Make the Winning Catch with Avon!

Script:
Convert your
Customers into
Avon
Representatives!

Call and ask your customer if she (or he!) is willing to take a brief over-the-phone customer survey in exchange for a spray bottle of Skin So Soft:

You: "Are you happy with the products so far?"

Note: Make sure to listen carefully to your customer's response. If there is a problem, now is the time to be a great Avon Rep and to answer her concerns. Problems should be few and far between - after all, we're talking about Avon!

You: "What are the benefits you've noticed?"

You: "Have your friends and family members noticed any positive change in you since using the products?"

You: "How else has Avon helped you?"

Then ask her (or him!) if she would like for you to show her a way that she can get the products at a big discount and/or earn some extra money in her spare time.

Set up an appointment! You've got a new recruit!

Top Ten Reasons David Letterman Needs an Avon Lady!

10. Add pizazz to your pencil toss with Avon Glimmersticks! It's America's number one eye-liner!

9. Raise your ratings in thirty days with Avon Lift and Tuck. "Tightens the tummy and lifts the rear in JUST 4 WEEKS!" (Weekly photo updates a must!)

8. To keep pesky guests from ever coming back, spritz yourself with Avon's Bug Guard Bug Repellent.

7. Add suspense to Will it Float with a capful of Avon Bubblebath. No one knows till the bubbles are gone!

6. Nail your jokes with the Avon 3-in-1 Manicure System.

5. For male guests with unruly nose and ear hair, live treatment with Avon Men's Personal Groomer. (Batteries not included)

4. Only your Avon Lady will know that you buy the Avon Skin So Soft Hair Removal Microwave Wax Kit for that out-of-control back hair problem. (Ouch!)

3. Free samples!

2. After jokes that tank, what could be better than Avon Cleanse for a refreshing "on air" body wash.

And the number reason why David Letterman needs an Avon Lady?

1. The next time Drew or Courtney are on the show - Dave, get ready with a tube of Avon Bust Sculpt. Applies in just twenty seconds!

Take Your Teamwork to the Streets!

21. Get your Avon Leadership team together - up-line and downline - and start or get involved in a charitable organization. Go out as a group and give Avon makeovers at a rehab center or nursing home. You will be changing hearts as well as getting folks interested in joining your team. It's a great way to sell some Avon, too!

A great way to get some returns? Start giving!

Come Highly Recommended!

22. This is a simple but extraordinarily effective tactic. Ask your recruits to write you a Letter of Recommendation. They could explain how selling Avon made them grow as a person, or perhaps allowed them to buy the car of their dreams. Maybe they simply love Avon products and are enjoying sharing Avon with others. Showing a prospective recruit a pile of recommendation letters is powerful! It's no longer just your word that Avon works - it's also the words of those you have already helped. If you are new to Avon and working on your first recruit, ask a couple of regular customers to write a letter for you.

Get them to tell their story!

Be a "T-ease"!

I love Avon!
Ask me Why!

23. Make a cute tee shirt that says "Ask Me About Selling Avon!" or "I Love Avon! Ask Me Why!" or "Looking For a Few Good Women!" What you wear can become a great conversation piece. Some people may laugh, but they will listen when you laugh, too, and then explain why you love selling Avon. Want to be the best upline ever? Make tee shirts for your recruits, and let them benefit, too!

"Ask Me About Selling Avon!"

Offer a Free Workshop!

24. Offer a Free Workshop on How To Generate A Home Income With a Beauty Business. You can advertise your workshop in the newspaper, through your place of worship, at the local unemployment office, and by placing flyers around town. Take reservations! Make sure you mention that Space is Limited. Offer free samples to attendees, as well as coffee, tea, and a simple snack like store-bought cookies. You can often rent a room at your library or community college for a small fee. Hand out copied sheets detailing how your students can earn money through Avon, whether by being a sales helper, by starting their own business and selling Avon, or through developing an Avon team through Leadership.

"How to Generate a Home Income with a Beauty Business"

Optimize Your Email!

25. Optimize your email signature. When you send an email to anyone, you can use the opportunity to advertise your Avon business and that you are looking for new recruits. Instead of simply signing with your name, add your contact information, and a couple of lines about how you sell Avon, and how they can sell Avon, too!

"Avon helps me with my bills, it could help with yours too!"

The Power of Storytelling!

26. The strongest and most wonderful tool you can use in your Avon recruiting efforts is your own story. Potential recruits want to know what it's really like selling Avon and building their own team. They don't want to hear the same old sales pitches telling them they will be rich. They want to hear the true ups and downs, the ways in which you succeeded, the ways in which you failed. Why not take a risk and open yourself up to being completely honest in your Avon Leadership business? When a potential recruit asks you what it's really like, TELL HER.

Share your ups and downs with potential recruits!

A Winning Combination!

27. Florists have a ready made clientele who love beautiful things. Why not add Avon products to their offerings? A bouquet and a bottle of Avon fragrance is better than a bunch of daisies! Add the tagline:

"Help Your Customers Bloom with Avon!"

Highlight One Product!

28. Start a biweekly Campaign Sample Club. Invite current customers and prospective new customers to join by giving you their email address. Send out an email each campaign highlighting an Avon product on sale in the brochure. List its benefits and tell your customers how it works for you or for those you know. Be specific! Invite your club members to call you for a free sample of the product, and give one lucky winner, randomly drawn, a full-sized product! Use this email to pitch your Avon business as as solution to their own needs.

Grow your email list!

Solve Your Potential Recruit's Problem!

29. The best way to recruit someone to your Avon team is to solve their problem. Don't tell them all the ways in which you rock! Don't tell them how much money they can make with Avon! Don't tell them how big a downline they can grow in 30 days. Spend a little time getting to know what questions they want answered, what problems they need solved. Maybe they need to figure out how to pay their cell phone bill each month. Maybe they need to make a few good friends and feel lonely. When you can identify what your potential recruit needs, you can figure out a way to help them solve their problem... through Avon.

Is Avon THEIR answer?

Avon is Golden!

30. Retirees: In this day and time, folks who retire from their primary career often need to find part time work in order to make ends meet. Retirees may also want something meaningful to do with their new found spare time. Avon can offer a wonderful opportunity to get out into the community and make new friends and acquaintances while filling one's pockets. Meet potential recruits at the local Senior Center. Post a flyer offering an opportunity to earn money toward a holiday cruise or a trip to see the grandkids.

"Retired? Restart your life with Avon!"

Feature Fido!

31. Make a blanket for your dog that goes over his or her body and advertises your Avon business. When you're out and about on a walk in the cool morning air, you may strike up a conversation with neighbors and passersby who are curious about your dog and Avon.

"Unleash Your Beauty and Business Potential!"

Put Avon on the Menu!

32. The Main Course: Some restaurants have menus where you can purchase a display ad. But better yet, talk to the owner and explain that this is the opportunity for her or him to use their own place to bring in even more business selling Avon. The ad can then be created for the restaurant owner:

"Today's Special is YOU!"

Reach Your Goal!

33. Tailgate at the next football or sports game, but instead of cooking hotdogs and burgers, set up an Avon display. Offer a full size product to anyone who signs up to sell! Explain that it only costs $10 to start an Avon business, and they can begin at the game! Hand them their kit and let them loose on the crowd!

Let them loose on the crowd!

Offer Free Reports!

34. Offer Free Reports on your blog or website: Give potential Avon Reps solid reasons why Avon will work for THEM. Ideas: *Free Report on How To Make a Recruiting Flier* or *Free Report on The Ten Best Avon Mascaras.* You can have folks fill out a request form to receive the Free Reports so that you can collect their name and email address. Follow up with a *Thank You for Downloading My Free Report* note, and ask if they have further questions about selling Avon.

Follow up with a Thank You!

Go Postal!

35. Get to know your postal carrier. He or she knows what's happening in your neighborhood! Someone's been laid off? Believe me, your postal carrier knows. Someone has a new baby? Someone's just retired? Give your postal carrier a generous supply of Avon samples from time to time and let him or her know that you both sell Avon and help others to sell it. Strike up a conversation when it's convenient, and you may be surprised at how helpful your postal carrier can be!

Your postal carier knows your neighborhood!

Be Facebook Friendly!

36. Do you know people who may want to learn more about Avon but aren't ready to commit? Invite them to friend you on Facebook. They can follow your adventures as you bring new members into your team and as you talk about Avon's most exciting new products. Be sure to post photos of yourself in Avon jewelry and clothing as well as makeup. Invite your Facebook friends to visit your Youravon.com page and order products, or to ask you about the Avon opportunity. You can even set up events such as Avon sale meetings and invite your Facebook friends.

"Friend Me on Facebook!"

Strech Your Body and Mind!

37. Yoga instructors, Pilates teachers, and Personal Trainers make excellent Avon Reps. They have an established list of clientele and meet hundreds of people a month through their business. People who work with your body learn about their client's personal lives, and can easily pinpoint those who could use another income avenue. Invite local bodyworkers to "Stretch Your Business" in an evening presentation. Hand out samples of Avon's skin care products and show your prospects the workout gear in your Avon brochures.

"Stretch Your Business!"

Who do YOU Know?

38. Ask every Avon customer if they know someone who could use some extra money. Everyone knows someone who is hurting in this economy. Even if your customer, family member, or friend isn't ready to sell Avon, he or she may know someone who is. Give every one of your friends, relatives, and customers a handful of your business cards to hand to those they meet who are looking for work.

Referrals can be an endless source of recruiting wealth!

Style Your Way to Riches!

39. Hairstylists are self-starters, used to working their own hours and finding their own clients. They are the ultimate go-getters! An Avon team full of hair stylists could be your "permanent" wealth solution. Hair stylists meet many clients a week, clients who might want a new look to go with their fresh locks. A combination Avon-Hair business is a win-win situation for many stylists. Drop by your favorite salon & talk to your own stylist first. Show her how Avon can multiply her earnings.

Hairstylists + Avon = Success!

Daycares Love AVON!

40. Women and men who operate daycare centers love Avon! Skin So Soft and other lotion products can save the day! Why not recruit daycare owners and workers into your downline? Most daycare centers and home-based programs have workers who could use an extra income stream. These people come into contact with many folks throughout the month, and could make a nice profit selling Avon.

"Baby yourself with Avon!"

Maintaining a Referral Network for Fun and Avon Profit!

Are you calling your friends, family, and customers and asking who they know who might want to sell Avon? Keep these ideas in mind when you recruit people to send you referrals:

Help your potential referrer - a friend, a co-worked, a customer, a family member - with memory joggers such as Who is your insurance agent? Who sold you your home? Whom do you know that is very health conscious? Who loves beauty products? Who cares about the environment? Who do you know that's a new mom?

Be clever! If the person offering referrals is a business person, offer a referral of your own! Find out all you can about the business - and passions - of the referring prospect and come up with ways to benefit that person in advance. They'll be sure and return your favors. For example, if your friend has a tire business, give them the name of a few good friends who could use a new set of Goodyears! Or, if they work in insurance, offer to get them in touch with a pair of newlyweds who may need life insurance!

Your referral will be ten times more likely to do business with you if you can get your referring friend to personally introduce you by telephone, email, or in person. Even Facebook can provide a wonderful change for you and your friends to meet like-minded folks! Even try Twitter! Linkedin.com is an especially fruitful way to meet folks interested in business.

You should reward activities that you want repeated. Whether the referral given to you comes through or not, show real appreciation to the person that gave you the referral. You don't have to offer money - you can offer Avon samples and products as Thank You. And, of course, at the very least, keep the referring person in the loop as to your progress each step of the way. Make building your business sound exciting! Your referrer may want to jump on the bandwagon herself!

Second-hand Can Put You in First Place!

41. Folks are cutting corners these days. It's a tough economy! Many people are looking for bargains at thrift stores. It's also an environmentally friendly way to shop. Why not bring a few small bottles of Avon's most loved products - Skin So Soft, Moisture Therapy, and one of the Avon Naturals lotions - and offer them to the independently-owned thrift store owner in exchange for leaving a pile of your carefully written flyers?

"Feeling Thrifty? Earn Money At Home With AVON!"

Reward Your Reps!

42. Avon offers stellar incentives for those who are successful recruiters, but why not add a reward system of your own? When one of your recruits brings someone onto your team, you both benefit. Offer a selection of Avon samples and demonstration products to those who bring prospects to the monthly Avon sales meetings, and a gift certificates for a nice dinner or a massage to those who close the deal. Everyone wins!

Let them know they're winners!

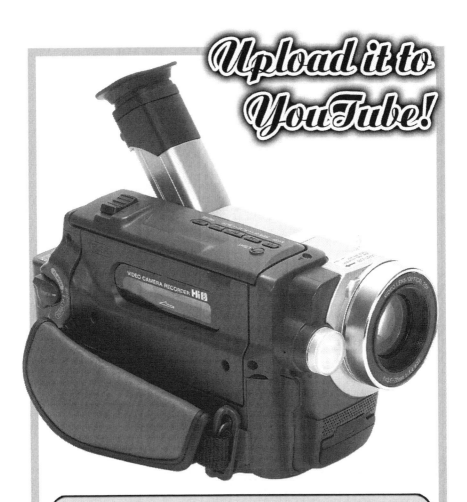

Upload it to YouTube!

43. Make your own recruitment video, just like the Air Force! It's okay if it's amateur and sloppy, just make it funny! Show your Leadership Team at a meeting or event. Show a few minutes of a typical Avon sales meeting, show your team members hanging out. The more hilarious, the better! You may even want to have a competition with your team to see who can put together the best recruitment video. Upload to YouTube!

The more hilarious, the better!

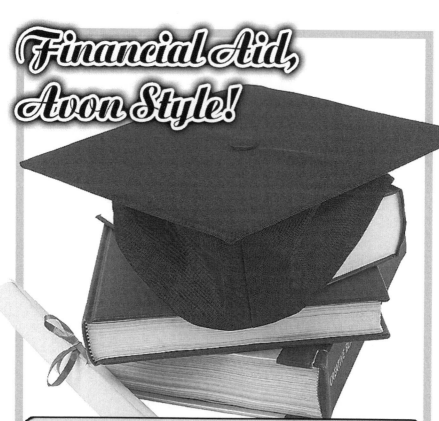

Financial Aid, Avon Style!

44. Have a Community College or a Four Year University in town? Every student is a possible recruit! Students aren't getting the comprehensive financial aid packages that they were just a few years ago, and with more educational cuts on the horizon, now is a great time to offer students a business of their own. Students have a built-in customer base: their classmates! Most higher education institutions have a Career Center where students can find information on local jobs. Drop by the center and bring business cards, Avon brochures, samples, and flyers that say:

"Need Money For School? Let Avon Help!"

The Avon Quiz!

45. Create a fun (and funny!) quiz about Avon! You can include questions about Avon's history, famous personalities, well-known products, and the ways in which a rep can earn through Avon. Make the quiz multiple choice, so that the test-taker has to choose which answer is correct. Hand out the quiz to prospective recruits. They will be surprised when they discover some exciting new facts about a company they might have thought they knew!

Show them fun Avon facts!

Be Aware of the Economic Forecast!

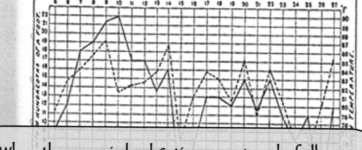

46. When the news is bad & times are tough, folks need money. An Avon business can put you back on your feet. Keep your eyes on the news. If you hear about a company closing, layoffs, be ready to share your Avon business with those affected by the downturn.

"Let Avon Help Put You Back on Your Feet!"

Sleep Your Way to Success!

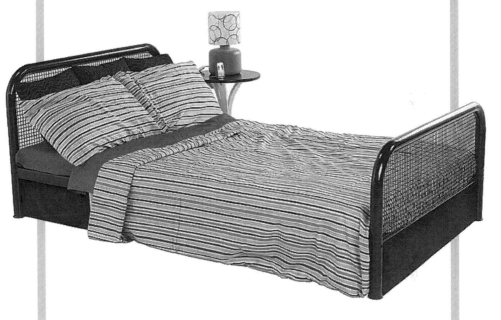

47. Bed-and-Breakfasts and locally owned Hotels often have proprietors who are looking for a second (or third!) income stream. These business owners work hard, and meet hundreds of new people a month, people who may need Avon products or another income stream themselves. Drop by these establishments with a little gift basket of useful samples - things that could be given to night guests - and start a conversation.

Open the door with a gift basket!

Avon Gift Basket Giveaways!

48. Buy a few attractive floral arrangement vases or fishbowls from your dollar store. Place them in local businesses - be sure to ask first - with a fancy sign explaining that a winner will be drawn once a month for a fabulous Avon gift basket. Invite folks to drop a business card in the bowl or to fill out a short form with their contact information. Call these folks and invite them to learn about Avon!

Invite Them to Learn About Avon!

List on Craigslist!

49. Use Craigslist in several ways: Craigslist.com is a boon for Avon Leadership candidates. Place a free ad in the Jobs section, explaining that you are an Avon Rep looking for other motivated, self-starting movers and shakers. These ads always work best if you include a personal testimonial. Be truthful! Tell your Craigslist audience how Avon has changed your life. Each ad on Craigslist receives hundreds if not thousands (sometimes more!) of views. Be creative! Don't forget to check the Looking for Work ads - you may find potential recruits begging for work.

Tell how Avon has changed your life!

Volunteer With the Junior League!

50. Most towns and cities have a Junior League, a group committed to helping young people learn about business. Get involved with the local youth business leaders and offer to teach short workshops on how to start a home-based business, how to organize a business, and how to make money through direct sales. These young people are your future recruits! If they are over 16, with parental permission, they can sell Avon and Avon's Mark line!

Young people are your future!

Ahead of the Herd!

51. Rescue an animal at the zoo or the animal shelter. Make a donation once a month and get your name on a plaque or in the zoo or shelter newsletter. Some things, like this, are for name recognition and community standing, and will help your name get Out There. If you are doing this, you can have a poster wherever you go, showing that you are saving animals.

"Our Elephant may be wrinkled, but you won't. Call us!"

Create a Newsletter!

52. Sometimes folks aren't ready to commit to a new business venture, but that doesn't mean that they don't hold an interest. Keep tabs on potential recruits via a newsletter. You can offer both print and e-versions of your updates. Make sure you send your newsletter out at regular increments - once a month is good. Mention any business awards you have won, levels you have achieved in Avon Leadership and Sales, promote your latest recruits, and talk about Avon's latest sales and newest products. Offer a coupon for a discount on a hot new skin care product - what a great way to re-connect with a customer and potential recruit. Always include a section on how any reader can become an Avon Rep through you.

Keep tabs on potential recruits once a month!

What Would Amelia Earhart Do?

53. A great idea for a recruiting poster: Pick a famous person from history, and make a top ten list of why she would make a great Avon Rep! Give your poster a vintage look and feel with old-timey fonts and colors. Create a series of these posters and hang them around town - you will get folks talking, and younger people will learn a bit of history, too!

"The woman who can create her own job is the woman who can win fame & fortune" - Amelia Earhart

Make Millions With Avon!

54. Blogging: You can generate fantastic leads for your business if you regularly blog about the fun and lucrative time you are having selling Avon. Set up a blog - there are many free services such as Blogger and Wordpress - and give it a positive name. How about "Make Millions With Avon" or "Your Avenue to Avon Success." Make sure you have an easy to use and find contact form or an email address so that interested persons can ask questions about selling Avon. Provide a special link to your contact info:

"Want to Make-Up with Your Bank Account? Contact Me!"

Look Them in the Eye!

55. Eye-level flyers or posters posted on bulletin boards can attract folks looking for an income stream. Community colleges, libraries, town halls, community centers, unemployment offices, and local stores are great places to tack up a thoughtful flyer. You can invite folks to an informational meeting using a flyer, or you can ask interested parties to contact you for information about selling Avon. Keep your flyers or posters neat, attractive, and easy to read.

Make sure your flyers are posted everywhere!

Throw a Party!

56. Not a sales party or a business party but a flat out fun social party! Invite all of your friends, relatives, co-workers, neighbors - everyone and anyone you know! Invite the cashier with the glowing smile! Invite the mechanic who takes care of your car. Enjoy yourself, have wonderful conversations, make new friends, visit with old ones, and gently tell folks that you are having a blast with your Avon business. Don't be pushy, don't try to recruit during the party, just enjoy. You may be surprised how many people want to hear MORE about what you are doing!

Invite everyone you know!

Place an Ad in Your Employee Newsletter!

57. Employee Newsletters and Publications sometimes allow workers to place classified ads. Ask if your workplace offers an opportunity to print a small ad for your outside-of-work business. Let your coworkers and employers know that you sell Avon, and that you can help them earn extra money in their own time at home.

Let your coworkers & employers know that you sell Avon!

Got the Relationship Blues?

58. Women fresh out of a long term relationship may have money issues. It can be scary going off on your own after years, even decades, of being in a partnership. If you know someone going through a big change in relationship life, invite them to look at Avon.

Invite them to partner with Avon!

Target the Top!

59. Having an Avon Leadership team can be exciting, but when every member of your organization is focused, self-starting, and sharp, your business will grow and grow - fast! Target the business leaders in your community - not those who are struggling to make ends meet (although those can be some of your best reps) - but those who are successful and know how to pull it all together. Invite the top business leaders in your community to a short seminar in which you show how their acumen and experience can send them to the top of Avon!

Aim for local business leaders!

Don't Give Up!

60. In a way, this is the most important "tip" in this book. Don't give up. Recruiting is a numbers game. You may meet the right people on the wrong day. You may meet the wrong people on the right day. You need to keep pushing ahead, keep making lists of potential recruits, keep using the techniques in this book to build your Avon business. Persistence and Love and Faith and Belief are what will help you reach your goals.

Success will come if you keep at it, rain or shine!

Five Ways to Write your OWN Recruiting Script!

1. Use an Outline!

Don't try to memorize an entire page or even a few paragraphs of text - even if your words are exciting. Come up with a basic outline that you can use when you call a potential recruit. You should always leave room for a little personal give-and-take. Maybe your potential recruit mentions that she enjoys bowling. If you stick to a rigid script, you won't get the change to ask her about her bowling league or whether she's thought about the ways in which her fellow bowlers could use Avon!

2. Keep it SHORT, baby! Everyone is busy these days! We are battling a tough economy, partners and children and parents who need our love and attention, and our own rewarding hobbies and interests. Most of us don't have time for an in-depth telephone call. Heck, most of us don't have time for a long email! You've seen the cute internet abbreviation: TL,DR which means Too Long, Didn't Read... Don't keep your potential recruits on the phone for more than a minute or two, and don't send long emails. Keep it short, sweet, and on topic.

3. Drop Names. Calling your friend's hairdresser? Use your friend's name. Calling a local politician? Tell her you sell Avon to the Mayor. Now is not the time to be coy. Use the names you know and love to help your potential recruit to see that she is part of a larger network. Everyone wants to be part of a group, especially one that's successful!

4. Tell your prospect... NO. Sounds silly, right? But it works! Let your potential recruit know that she is probably Too Busy, or Doesn't Have an Interest in a Home Business, or that she may not be the Right Person to Speak With. Your prospect will be caught off guard, and won't see you as being pushing or aggressive. She will pursue YOU!

5. Value is Queen. Early in the conversation or email - and I personally recommend having a person one-on-one conversation - you should tell your potential Avon recruit why she or he is benefitted by working with you. Tell her that you spend ten hours a week training new recruits, or that you offer a weekly newsletter to inspire and inform new Avon Reps. Let your recruit know why YOUR downline is THE downline to join!

Your Own Customers!

61. The folks who regularly purchase Avon products from you can be your best recruits! They already believe in the power of Avon to transform their body - why not invite them to transform their pocketbook, too? Share the ways in which they can both save money on their own favorite skin care regimen, lipsticks, and body care products, as well as share the Avon world with others through sales and recruiting.

"Transform Your Pocketbook!"

Temporary Tatoos!

Got Lipstick?

62. This sounds a little crazy, but it works! Have some temporary tattoos made up (google for companies that do this - it's not expensive!) and hand them out! Make them fun, a little irreverent. "*Got Soap?*" or "*Lipstick Diva*" is a cute way to bring attention to your Avon business.

Bring attention to your Avon Business!

Tweet - But Don't SPAM!

63. It's easy to get into SPAM mode, where you tweet and chat and Facebook the same thing over and over, hoping that someone will want to join your Leadership team. That never works! It's best to come up with a unique and personal twist, and to tell your own story using modern social media. Use Twitter to make your followers aware of what's happening in your Avon business world. Instead of tweeting "Join my Avon team today!" why not try something like "I just recruited a wonderful mother of three in Chicago. She loves Skin So Soft & hopes to earn $50 her first campaign!" See how much more engaging the second tweet is? Be creative!

Tell your exciting Avon news!

Waiting Rooms Hold Captive Audiences!

64. Most Avon Reps stamp their brochures with the slogan "To buy or sell Avon, call..." This may be enough to bring in a few recruits a year. Ramp up your incoming prospect calls by inserting a fun flyer into the brochures you already leave in waiting rooms. Folks stuck at the doctor or dentist love looking through the latest Avon brochures. Be sure to keep the waiting rooms well-stocked with fresh brochures. Include a bookmark in each brochure that says "Call me for free samples!" and includes your telephone number. Tuck in a folded flyer that lists a few benefits of building an Avon business.

List the benefits of bulding an Avon business!

Baby and Me and Avon!

65. New Moms: Know someone who is having a baby? She could be your next recruit! Why not invite expecting and new mothers to earn a little extra spending money while they are home with their new arrival? Selling Avon can take just a few minutes out of her busy day, but the rewards can be big. Why not grow a business along with your little one? Avon's baby care line and the new Tiny Tilla clothing and accessory line can help a new mom share products and the Avon sales experience with other new moms she meets at Lamaze and Baby and Me classes!

Mom could be your next recruit!

Letters to Businesses!

66. Many small business owners are hurting in our current economy and would welcome an opportunity to build a new income stream. Write personal letters to every small business in your community, inviting them to hear more about your Avon business. Tell your own stories in your letter - explain the ways in which Avon has allowed you to save money for a downpayment on a car or home, talk about the improved confidence and personal pride you feel. The more personal the letter, the more it will affect the reader. Give a few short examples in your letter as to how their particular business could benefit through Avon.

Tell your own stories in your letter- make it personal!

Don't Just Say "Thank You!"

67. Are you driving a new car thanks to your Unit Leader bonus check? Were you just profiled in your local paper because of a successful charity campaign? Did you just close on a new condo thanks to making Rose Circle? When someone compliments you or congratulates you, don't just say Thank You, tell them HOW you accomplished your goal through Avon!

Make sure that the people in your life know HOW Avon is working for you!

Hit the Road with Your Business!

68. Adopt a highway, or a bench, or buy a brick in a new facility. It's another way to get your name out there, and you can use it in your marketing materials:

"Everyone Needs a Good Foundation!"

Take Your Team to the (Job) Fair!

69. Does your city host a job fair? If so, get your down-line together and splurge on a table at the event. Sign up your team members to work different shifts during the fair. Hand out lots of samples and brochures ~ you can gain customers as well as reps ~ and hold a free drawing for an Avon gift basket filled with the latest and greatest Avon products! Make sure you get every visitor's name and email address ~ a phone number, too, if you can ~ so that you can follow up after the fair. Split the list with your participating downline! What a fun way show a little team spirit and grow your business together!

Hand out samples & brochures!

Reverse Psycghology!

70. Turn Avon on its head! Have some fun with this one by being a bit silly - Make a poster or a flyer explaining why no one should be an Avon Rep! Some examples: "Why bother having soft, silky legs with *Skin So Soft* when you can show off your itchy flea-bitten gams?" or "Over 50 scents of delightful Avon deodorants? No thanks, I'd rather smell like Oscar the Grouch!"

Get their Attention!

You Already Know a Small Army!

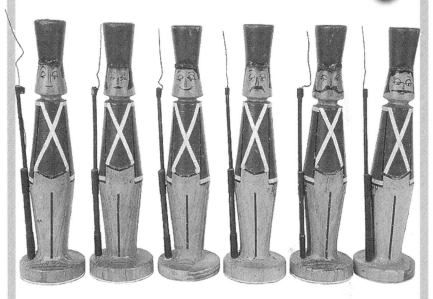

71. You already know a small army of folks who inter-act with the public! Housecleaners! Landscapers! Pet sitters! These people come to your home - and many others' homes - and would be wonderful add-itions to your Avon sales team. They already know the buying and beauty habits of their own customers. Why not help them expand into the beauty arena? Those who work for themselves usually are open to new business opportunities, too.

Avon makes a great additional business for self-starters!

Raise Money for the Humane Society!

72. Offer to host an Avon fundraiser for one of your favorite organizations. How about raising money for Boy Scouts or the local Humane Society? Your hard work and efforts will not go unnoticed, and the feel good vibes that folks get from your Avon products will give you you a positive position in their mind. Follow up with patrons who purchase your products and ask if they want to hear about the Avon opportunity.

Your hard work and efforts will not go unnoticed!

Cruise the Classifieds!

73. Where do folks go who need to find a job? The classified ads in the local newspaper! A small investment in a series of "Earn Money With Avon" ads can reap great rewards. If you have a blog, make sure you list your URL in the ad. Good phrases to use in your ad include "Work At Home," "Beauty Careers," and "Work For Yourself." Leave your phone number and an email address!

"Work at Home Beauty Career!"

Teach Yourself Beauty!

74. Teachers are some of our most important - and most underpaid - community members. Teachers usually keep seasonal hours, too, working during the school year and having several months off during the summer during which they could sell Avon. Teachers also know hundreds of parents! Target the teachers in your area schools with a flyer that says:

"Learn How to Educate Others About Beauty!"

Sign Up For Success!

AVON Rocks- Ask me WHY!

555-1213

75. Exchange a free Avon product or two with your friends, co-workers, or neighbors in exchange for allowing a yard sign with your business name and telephone number. *"Buy and Sell Skin So Soft"* or *"Avon Rocks - Ask Me Why!"* Choose homes that are in heavily traveled areas.

"Buy and Sell Skin so Soft!"

Create a New Recruit' Kit!

My Avon Team Kit

76. Sure, Avon has a wonderful kit for new Sales Reps, but how about adding your own Team Kit for new recruits? Add a team calendar, team tee shirt or key chain, a handbook of team members' contact information, a small gift certificate for a meal out, all in a team tote bag. It's exciting starting your own business, and if you feel like you are part of a vibrant team that's really going places, you are more likely to stick with it and want to be a valuable team member.

Help your new Team Members feel like they are going places!

An 'Elevator Speech' Will Raise You Up!

77. An "elevator speech" is a three minute description of your business that you could give to someone while stuck on an elevator. Developing and practicing an elevator speech is a great way to have on the tip of your tongue a quick, to-the-point, fun, exciting description that can instantly interest your listener in your Avon business. Write out your elevator speech and practice it in front of a mirror. The next time someone asks you, "So, what do you do?" you will be ready!

"So, what do you do?"

Beginner's Mind!

78. Every potential new recruit feels overwhelmed when they look at the huge array of products Avon regularly offers, as well as the different kinds of ways a rep can earn an income. Make it easy for interested folks by creating a simple info-graphic or flow chart showing how easy it is to share brochures and samples, collect orders, distribute product, and invite others to do the same. A picture can say a thousand words. Use your own experience and location to create a cool graphic that will work in your area.

Potential recruits may feel overwhelmed!

Radio Avon!

79. Most communities have a local radio station that invites communities businesspeople to tell their stories on air. Listen to the station to get an idea of what folks are discussing, and call in to arrange your own interview. Be prepared - come with a list of highlights of your Avon career. Tell funny stories about the kind customers you have met along the way. Tell your audience how Avon helped you buy a new car or pay for your daughter's college education. Be specific. Describe some of your favorite products. Make sure you give listeners a way to contact you - a website, a phone number, an email address.

Tell your Avon story on the air!

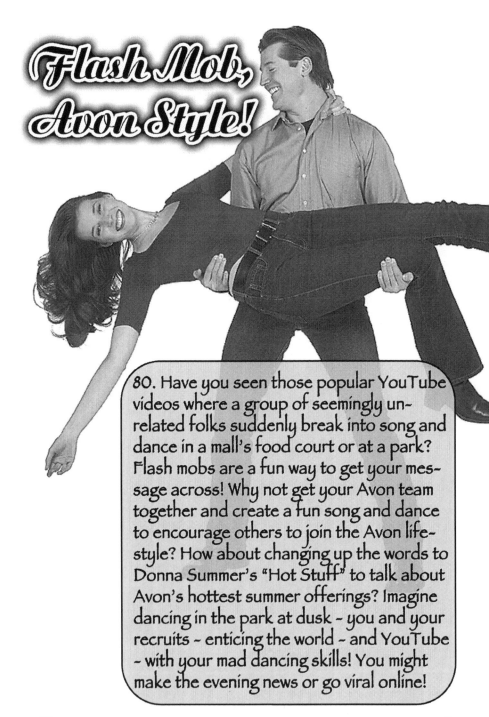

Flash Mob, Avon Style!

80. Have you seen those popular YouTube videos where a group of seemingly un-related folks suddenly break into song and dance in a mall's food court or at a park? Flash mobs are a fun way to get your message across! Why not get your Avon team together and create a fun song and dance to encourage others to join the Avon life-style? How about changing up the words to Donna Summer's "Hot Stuff" to talk about Avon's hottest summer offerings? Imagine dancing in the park at dusk - you and your recruits - enticing the world - and YouTube - with your mad dancing skills! You might make the evening news or go viral online!

Dance your way to success!

How to Keep Your New Recruits

Do you find that your Avon Representatives disappear faster than the ink dries on their application?

Now that you're building your downline using 100 Ways to Recruit, and training them how to sell using 100 Ways to Sell Avon, use the motivational techniques in my upcoming book How To Keep Your Avon Recruits to keep your downline motivated, excited, and working toward their own goals as they build their OWN downline!

Here are a couple of ideas to get you started:

Welcome all new recruits!

Send a personal welcome to each of your new recruits, and your downline members' new recruits - regardless of how far down the chain they may be. Let them know where to find Avon's best training tools. Personally hand each new recruit a calendar of your Team's meetings and order and delivery dates. Make yourself available to help them get started on the right path. Be sure to praise the person who recruited them so that they know they are on a winning team! You never know which of your downline will be the next Avon Superstar!

Keep in touch

Personally contact each of your team members and see how they are doing at least once each month. This is a good idea even if some in your team are making sales and recruiting representatives without your help. Just check in and see if anyone has questions or problems - they may be afraid to ask for help. By taking that first step, your downline will be more likely to succeed. Your team will know that they can rely on you to assist them, and will look forward to impressing you when you make that monthly call!

Provide Child Care!

81. Moms with little children may be interested in selling Avon, but feel as if they wouldn't be able to attend Avon Sales Meetings, or even be able to meet you at a public location to hear about the Avon opportunity. Some moms may not feel that they can invite someone over to their home if they are busy chasing toddlers all day. Why not host a morning information meeting & offer free child care?

Access the New Mom network!

Write a Guest Column!

82. Be My Guest: Offer to write a guest column for your newspaper or for a beauty blog! The media eats content – every day, newspapers and blogs need to come up with thousands of words to entertain their rabid fans. Why not have YOUR words be chosen? Write a 500 word article on why selling Avon can change your life and line your pocket, and submit it to your local paper or your favorite beauty blog. Make sure you add your contact info to your bio! Come up with some fun angles: Perhaps "The Top Ten Reasons You Should Sell Avon," or "How to Solve Your Budget Crunch with Avon."

"Solve Your Budget Crunch with Avon!"

Make Sure You Are Listed!

83. Telephone Books are quickly becoming an anachronism. It won't be long until these dinosaurs are strictly online. But while they still exist, they are a great way to get the word out that you own a business that is growing and looking for new blood! Place a display ad with your telephone number. Make sure you are listed under Avon and under Cosmetics.

"Buy or Sell Avon - Call Me!"

Make an Avonopoly Game!

84. Take a Monopoly Game that you buy at a yard sale and change it to Avonopoly. Glue tags over Park Place, Indiana Avenue, and all of the properties to say things like *Skin So Soft Park, Avon Naturals Place, Anew Avenue*. Invite potential recruits over for a fun game of Avonopoly at a local coffee shop. Winner gets a gift basket of Avon goodies. Talk about the fun you have selling Avon while you play the game.

Skin So Soft Park and Anew Avenue!

Demonstration-a-thon!

85. Your customers may be used to getting to sample several products each campaign, but what if they could see the wide array of Avon body care products, makeup, jewelry, clothes, and houseware items all at once? Remember how excited you were when you attended your first Home for the Holidays conference and could touch, see, smell, and hear every product in the Christmas line? Hold a Demonstration-a-thon with your Avon Leadership team. Get your recruits together and divide and conquer. Each team member wears Avon, and brings up to 10 full sized products to demo. Hold the event in someone's home or rent a small space for the evening. Invite customers and prospective recruits to:

"Sample All Avon Has to Offer!"

Bat Your Way to Big Earnings!

86. Get your Avon Leadership team together and start a bowling team or a softball team! Join the local leagues and get in on the action! This is a fantastic way to stay in shape and keep in the social loop. You can share recruiting techniques with your downline and upline, as well as get folks on other teams interested in your business.

Your Avon Leadership team will hit a home run!

Make Your Avon Sales Meetings Interactive!

87. Sure, you managed to drag a few folks to your monthly sales meeting, but what happens once you get them there? You haven't recruited them until they've signed the papers and picked up their Avon kit. Speak with your District Manager about changing up the meetings. Most DMs are incredible and know how to work a crowd. They love to give out samples and door prizes, and are wonderful teachers! But why not try something outside the box? How about musical chairs, with a nice Avon jewelry box taped beneath one chair? How about breaking the larger group up into smaller groups, each with a Unit Leader who can inspire with some real-life stories? Getting folks to move about the room will keep attention focused and attitudes high!

Try something outside the box!

Find Top Notch Members!

88. People who put resumes together for others can be top notch Avon team members. These people come into contact with those looking for work every single day. When they meet someone whose experience looks like it may be a good fit for Avon, they can offer the opportunity. The wonderful thing about selling Avon and building an Avon team is that it can be done part time!

Make connections with folks looking for work!

Set Up a Team Webpage!

89. Set up a Team Webpage for your Leadership Team: Get a descriptive URL, perhaps GoNYCAvonWildCatsGo.com, where your downline can post their successes and sales advice. Potential new recruits will get excited seeing how busy your team is, and your own members will find inspiration in each other's good works. Little things like this make a huge difference in team energy and support!

Pump up your team energy!

Teach a Workshop!

COMPANY

90. In some areas of the country, a company called Learning Annex lets entrepreneurs set up low-cost workshops which get marketed to a huge audience interested in business and personal programs. Your community may have Learning Annex or something similar. Approach them with your idea: You will provide a two hour beauty workshop - perhaps *"How to Dress for a Job Interview."* You will be teaching folks who are looking for work - your target audience - and showing them Avon's clothing, jewelry, and makeup!

"How to Dress for an Interview."

Bump Your Way to Success!

AVON ON BOARD!

91. When you're stuck in slow moving traffic, what has your attention? The bumper in front of you, of course! Put your own advertising space to good use and create a clever bumper sticker for your Avon business. This is especially effective if you are in traffic during rush hour. *"If you worked for yourself you wouldn't be reading this today."*

Don't forget a phone number!

When the Money is Thin...

92. We all know folks who have financial obstacles. Some people who may be open to the Avon earning opportunity include: those with outstanding medical bills, moms whose children are starting college, anyone whose spouse has been laid off, a friend with car trouble. In today's world, more than one income is needed to make ends meet, and sometimes a family needs several avenues of income. Don't be shy - let your friends and acquaintances know that you can help by assisting them with an Avon business.

"Feeling the Financial Squeeze? Avon Can Help!"

Baby Steps!

93. Some folks may be interested in selling Avon, but may be too timid to give it a whirl. Consider taking them on as a helper. Offer them a generous discount on products or a commission on sales they bring to you. Once they realize how easy it is to sell Avon, they will want to become a full fledged rep! By being a considering, caring, and understanding Avon Leadership rep, you will help others to help themselves.

Let people participate at their own comfort level!

Artists and Musicians Make Great Reps!

94. Artists and Musicians are some of the most important people in our communities. Their work brings light and joy to our lives, but most creative folks don't earn enough income to meet their needs or goals. Make a list of all of the artists and musicians you know. Create a flyer that features:

"Income Generation for Creatives!"

Business Cards!

95. Don't forget some of the most time-tested and proven of all business recruiting techniques! Business cards can do so much more than convey your name and contact information. Use your cards to tell a story using short, fun phrases and unforgettable images. Print a photo of your favorite Avon lipstick and a dollar bill and add the tagline:

"Ruby Red + Soft Coral = GREEN!"

Uplift Yourself, Union Style!

96. Unions and Trade Organizations are full of people who work hard to uplift and assist the lives of others. Get to know your local Union, and let them know that you sell Avon and would be pleased to present the Avon earnings opportunity to any displaced workers or those who are looking for some additional income.

Avon is a great choice for displaced workers!

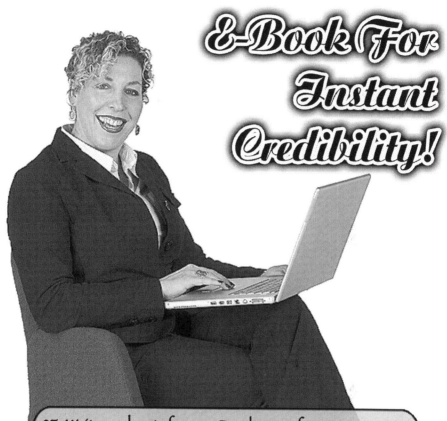

E-Book For Instant Credibility!

97. Write a short, free e-Book on a fun Avon topic. How about *"20 Uses for Avon Mascara"* or *"Three Ways to Demonstrate Your Favorite Fragrance"* - a book makes you an instant expert. Others looking for someone to sell Avon under, will want someone who knows how to sell and how to relate that information to a new recruit. You can place a link to download your free e-Book on your blog or website. You can also link to it on your youravon.com site! Tell the world that You Know Avon!

"Three Ways to Demonstrate Your Favorite Fragrance!"

Who Do You Know That is Looking to Buy a New Car?

98. More Who Do You Know to kick start your recruiting efforts: Who do you know who is bored? Who do you know who wants a promotion at their work? Who do you know who is looking to buy a new car? Which of your customers enjoys your product demonstrations the most? Which of your customers always orders the most product?

You already know your next Recruit!

Float Your Beauty Boat!

99. Every community has several parades throughout the year! Why not get your Avon downline together and create a float for a local charity? What a beautiful way to get your message across to thousands of cheering fans! You can toss Avon samples instead of candy! Build a float for the Children's Hospital, or for Breast Cancer Awareness. Make sure your sign mentions your Avon team and how someone can get involved. This is a great way to find yourself on the television news and in the newspaper, too!

Become the face of Avon in your community!

Cowboy Up!

100. Put up a booth or table at the County Fair or Rodeo! Is your community holding a health fair? Put up a booth sharing some of Avon's gentle products! Collect names and contact information, and follow up with visitors, inviting them to attend a free workshop or to try Avon's latest samples. Offer face painting at your booth and attract moms with young children, or sponsor a dunking booth - dunk the Avon Lady for a chance to win a gift basket! Have some fun!

Offer Facepainting or one-minute makeovers!

About the Author

Birdie Jaworski lives and writes in New Mexico.

Birdie's memoir of her time selling women's cosmetics door-to-door, "Don't Shoot! I'm Just the Avon Lady!" was nominated for a Pushcart Award.

Birdie's collection of real-life short stories set in rural New Mexico, "My Tiny Vegas," includes stories about the secret Scientology mesa outside of Las Vegas, New Mexico, as well as heartwarming stories about green chile, santeros, and life on the edge of the Great Plains.

You can visit Birdie's website at birdiejaworski.com.

More Books from Birdie!

100 Ways to Sell Avon helps you build your Avon business with fun, tested ways of getting your Avon brochures into customer's hands. Includes tips on how to use your Avon eRep site, how to use Social Media to build your Avon business as well as fun stories about real life Avon Representative adventures from well-known Avon Lady blogger Birdie Jaworski. 100 Ways to Sell Avon will help you jump start your Avon sales! This is a fun and accessible way to get the sales information you need to be successful! The book is easy to read and has fun graphics illustrating each of the 100 ways, sprinkled with hilarious stories from a real Avon Rep. Lots of other marketing tips from How to Go Green to Making Homemade Business Cards! Sell Avon? Get this book!

My Tiny Vegas: Birdie Jaworski lives on the edge of the eastern plains of New Mexico, where the Sangre de Christo Mountains meet the Great Plains, smack in the middle of the town of Las Vegas. No - not the big City of Sin with the gambling strip! Las Vegas, New Mexico is not as well known as other Wild West towns, such as Dodge City, Deadwood, or Tombstone, but she is said to have been the worst of the rowdiest Old West towns. She's still rowdy, still mysterious, still full of larger-than-life characters! Doc Holliday kept his medical office in Las Vegas, New Mexico. The Rough Riders held their first reunion in the saloon of the Plaza Hotel in Las Vegas. You can get a shot of tequila in that same saloon, today. Let Birdie share her beautiful tiny Las Vegas with you..

• And look for *How To Keep Your Avon Recruits*, due out in 2013, with tons of tips and fun stories to give you information and motivation to help you take your Avon business to the next level!

Made in the USA
Lexington, KY
21 November 2012